Francis Frith's
STAFFORDSHIRE

PHOTOGRAPHIC MEMORIES

Francis Frith's
STAFFORDSHIRE

◆

Clive Hardy

FRITH
BOOK Co

First published in the United Kingdom in 1999 by
Frith Book Company Ltd

Hardback Edition
ISBN 1-85937-047-0

Paperback Edition 2001
ISBN 1-85937-308-9

British Library Cataloguing in Publication Data

Francis Frith's Staffordshire
Clive Hardy

Frith Book Company Ltd
Frith's Barn, Teffont,
Salisbury, Wiltshire SP3 5QP
Tel: +44 (0) 1722 716 376
Email: info@francisfrith.co.uk
www.francisfrith.co.uk

Printed and bound in Great Britain

CONTENTS

FRANCIS FRITH: *Victorian Pioneer*

FRANCIS FRITH, Victorian founder of the world-famous photographic archive, was a complex and multitudinous man. A devout Quaker and a highly successful Victorian businessman, he was both philosophic by nature and pioneering in outlook.

By 1855 Francis Frith had already established a wholesale grocery business in Liverpool, and sold it for the astonishing sum of £200,000, which is the equivalent today of over £15,000,000. Now a multi-millionaire, he was able to indulge his passion for travel. As a child he had pored over travel books written by early explorers, and his fancy and imagination had been stirred by family holidays to the sublime mountain regions of Wales and Scotland. 'What a land of spirit-stirring and enriching scenes and places!' he had written. He was to return to these scenes of grandeur in later years to 'recapture the thousands of vivid and tender memories', but with a different purpose. Now in his thirties, and captivated by the new science of photography, Frith set out on a series of pioneering journeys to the Nile regions that occupied him from 1856 until 1860.

INTRIGUE AND ADVENTURE

He took with him on his travels a specially-designed wicker carriage that acted as both dark-room and sleeping chamber. These far-flung journeys were packed with intrigue and adventure. In his life story, written when he was sixty-three, Frith tells of being held captive by bandits, and of fighting 'an awful midnight battle to the very point of surrender with a deadly pack of hungry, wild dogs'. Sporting flowing Arab costume, Frith arrived at Akaba by camel seventy years before Lawrence, where he encountered 'desert princes and rival sheikhs, blazing with jewel-hilted swords'.

During these extraordinary adventures he was assiduously exploring the desert regions bordering the Nile and patiently recording the antiquities and peoples with his camera. He was the first photographer to venture beyond the sixth cataract. Africa was still the mysterious 'Dark Continent', and Stanley and Livingstone's historic meeting was a decade into the future. The conditions for picture taking confound belief. He laboured for hours in his wicker dark-room in the sweltering heat of the desert, while the volatile chemicals fizzed dangerously in their trays. Often he was forced to work in remote tombs and caves where conditions were cooler. Back in London he exhibited his photographs and was 'rapturously cheered' by members of the Royal Society. His reputation as a photographer was made overnight. An eminent modern historian has likened their impact on the population of the time to that on our own generation of the first photographs taken on the surface of the moon.

VENTURE OF A LIFE-TIME

Characteristically, Frith quickly spotted the opportunity to create a new business as a specialist publisher of photographs. He lived in an era of immense and sometimes violent change. For the poor in the early part of Victoria's reign work was a drudge and the hours long, and people had precious little free time to enjoy themselves.

Most had no transport other than a cart or gig at their disposal, and had not travelled far beyond the boundaries of their own town or village. However, by the 1870s, the railways had threaded their way across the country, and Bank Holidays and half-day Saturdays had been made obligatory by Act of Parliament. All of a sudden the ordinary working man and his family were able to enjoy days out and see a little more of the world.

With characteristic business acumen, Francis Frith foresaw that these new tourists would enjoy having souvenirs to commemorate their days out. In 1860 he married Mary Ann Rosling and set out with the intention of photographing every city, town and village in Britain. For the next thirty years he travelled the country by train and by pony and trap, producing fine photographs of seaside resorts and beauty spots that were keenly bought by millions of Victorians. These prints were painstakingly pasted into family albums and pored over during the dark nights of winter, rekindling precious memories of summer excursions.

THE RISE OF FRITH & CO

Frith's studio was soon supplying retail shops all over the country. To meet the demand he gathered about him a small team of photographers, and published the work of independent artist-photographers of the calibre of Roger Fenton and Francis Bedford. In order to gain some understanding of the scale of Frith's business one only has to look at the catalogue issued by Frith & Co in 1886: it runs to some 670

pages, listing not only many thousands of views of the British Isles but also many photographs of most European countries, and China, Japan, the USA and Canada – note the sample page shown above from the hand-written *Frith & Co* ledgers detailing pictures taken. By 1890 Frith had created the greatest specialist photographic publishing company in the world, with over 2,000 outlets – more than the combined number that Boots and WH Smith have today! The picture on the right shows the *Frith & Co* display board at Ingleton in the Yorkshire Dales. Beautifully constructed with mahogany frame and gilt inserts, it could display up to a dozen local scenes.

POSTCARD BONANZA
◆

The ever-popular holiday postcard we know today took many years to develop. In 1870 the Post Office issued the first plain cards, with a pre-printed stamp on one face. In 1894 they allowed other publishers' cards to be sent through the mail with an attached adhesive halfpenny stamp. Demand grew rapidly, and in 1895 a new size of postcard was permitted called the

court card, but there was little room for illustration. In 1899, a year after Frith's death, a new card measuring 5.5 x 3.5 inches became the standard format, but it was not until 1902 that the divided back came into being, with address and message on one face and a full-size illustration on the other. *Frith & Co* were in the vanguard of postcard development, and Frith's sons Eustace and Cyril continued their father's monumental task, expanding the number of views offered to the public and recording more and more places in Britain, as the coasts and countryside were opened up to mass travel.

Francis Frith died in 1898 at his villa in Cannes, his great project still growing. The archive he created continued in business for another seventy years. By 1970 it contained over a third of a million pictures of 7,000 cities, towns and villages. The massive photographic record Frith has left to us stands as a living monument to a special and very remarkable man.

Frith's Archive: *A Unique Legacy*

FRANCIS FRITH'S legacy to us today is of immense significance and value, for the magnificent archive of evocative photographs he created provides a unique record of change in 7,000 cities, towns and villages throughout Britain over a century and more. Frith and his fellow studio photographers revisited locations many times down the years to update their views, compiling for us an enthralling and colourful pageant of British life and character.

We tend to think of Frith's sepia views of Britain as nostalgic, for most of us use them to conjure up memories of places in our own lives with which we have family associations. It often makes us forget that to Francis Frith they were records of daily life as it was actually being lived in the cities, towns and villages of his day. The Victorian age was one of great and often bewildering change for ordinary people, and though the pictures evoke an impression of slower times, life was as busy and hectic as it is today.

We are fortunate that Frith was a photographer of the people, dedicated to recording the minutiae of everyday life. For it is this sheer wealth of visual data, the painstaking chronicle of changes in dress, transport, street layouts, buildings, housing, engineering and landscape that captivates us so much today. His remarkable images offer us a powerful link with the past and with the lives of our ancestors.

TODAY'S TECHNOLOGY

Computers have now made it possible for Frith's many thousands of images to be accessed almost instantly. In the Frith archive today, each photograph is carefully 'digitised' then stored on a CD Rom. Frith archivists can locate a single photograph amongst thousands within seconds. Views can be catalogued and sorted under a variety of categories of place and content to the immediate benefit of researchers. Inexpensive reference prints can be created for them at the touch of a mouse button, and a wide range of books and other printed materials assembled and published for a wider, more general readership - in the next twelve months over a hundred Frith local history titles will be published! The

See Frith at www. francisfrith.co.uk

day-to-day workings of the archive are very different from how they were in Francis Frith's time: imagine the herculean task of sorting through eleven tons of glass negatives as Frith had to do to locate a particular sequence of pictures! Yet the archive still prides itself on maintaining the same high standards of excellence laid down by Francis Frith, including the painstaking cataloguing and indexing of every view.

It is curious to reflect on how the internet now allows researchers in America and elsewhere greater instant access to the archive than Frith himself ever enjoyed. Many thousands of individual views can be called up on screen within seconds on one of the Frith internet sites, enabling people living continents away to revisit the streets of their ancestral home town, or view places in Britain where they have enjoyed holidays. Many overseas researchers welcome the chance to view special theme selections, such as transport, sports, costume and ancient monuments.

We are certain that Francis Frith would have heartily approved of these modern developments, for he himself was always working at the very limits of Victorian photographic technology.

THE VALUE OF THE ARCHIVE TODAY

Because of the benefits brought by the computer, Frith's images are increasingly studied by social historians, by researchers into genealogy and ancestory, by architects, town planners, and by teachers and schoolchildren involved in local history projects. In addition, the archive offers every one of us a unique opportunity to examine the places where we and our families have lived and worked down the years. Immensely successful in Frith's own era, the archive is now, a century and more on, entering a new phase of popularity.

THE PAST IN TUNE WITH THE FUTURE

Historians consider the Francis Frith Collection to be of prime national importance. It is the only archive of its kind remaining in private ownership and has been valued at a million pounds. However, this figure is now rapidly increasing as digital technology enables more and more people around the world to enjoy its benefits.

Francis Frith's archive is now housed in an historic timber barn in the beautiful village of Teffont in Wiltshire. Its founder would not recognize the archive office as it is today. In place of the many thousands of dusty boxes containing glass plate negatives and an all-pervading odour of photographic chemicals, there are now ranks of computer screens. He would be amazed to watch his images travelling round the world at unimaginable speeds through network and internet lines.

The archive's future is both bright and exciting. Francis Frith, with his unshakeable belief in making photographs available to the greatest number of people, would undoubtedly approve of what is being done today with his lifetime's work. His photographs, depicting our shared past, are now bringing pleasure and enlightenment to millions around the world a century and more after his death.

STAFFORDSHIRE – *An Introduction*

THE LAND-LOCKED, midlands county of Staffordshire is bordered by Cheshire, Derbyshire, Warwickshire, Worcestershire, Shropshire, and is just kissed by Leicestershire. The highest points are in the Moorlands area, which is an extension of the Derbyshire Peak District, famed for its rugged and often bleak scenery. Here the Roaches rise to 1,657ft, and Merryton Law to 1,603ft, nearly twice the height of the highest ground on Cannock Chase.

Just when Staffordshire was first named is unclear, but it was probably around AD920 when Edward the Elder of Wessex deposed his niece Aelfwyn to take the Mercian throne. Edward, helped by his sister Ethelfleda of Mercia, had not only successfully repelled an all-out Danish attack in AD910, but had gone on the offensive, so that by AD920 a part of the Danelaw had been reconquered and Northumbria had recognized him as overlord. Edward, however, did not have things entirely his own way. In AD922 the Mercians of Cheshire and their Welsh allies were in armed revolt, and still were so when Edward died at Farndon in AD924.

During Ethelred the Unready's reign, Cheshire, Staffordshire and Shropshire became what was in effect an independent land, ruled by the Earls of Mercia, free from royal control. Apart from an attempt by Edmund Ironside to restore the royal writ, the three counties enjoyed their autonomous status until the eve of the Norman Conquest.

During the 12th and 13th centuries the population of the county grew steadily, but with few roads and a lack of navigable rivers, trade and growth were hindered for several centuries. None the less, industry had taken hold; it would be in pottery, coal and iron that the county would excel. By the 10th century pottery was being manufactured in and around Stafford, but it would be Burslem that would rise to become the main centre of this industry during the 13th and 14th centuries. By the mid to late 13th century, forges were established at Cannock, Rugeley and Sedgley. These early forges smelted iron ore in a bloomery, which was often little more than an open hearth fired by charcoal. By Tudor times, the first blast furnaces were being introduced; the blast was provided by water powered bellows. Water wheels also provided the motive power for the early drop hammers and the first slitting mills, which cut iron rods into workable lengths for nail makers.

The real advance in the iron smelting industry came in the early 18th century with the use of coke. The pioneer in Staffordshire was John Wilkinson, who opened a coke-fired smelter at Bradley, near Bilston, in 1757. By the end of the Napoleonic Wars there were more than fifty coke-fired blast furnaces operating in the county with an annual output in excess of 110,000 tonnes.

Staffordshire, however, was especially rich in coal. In the north of the county, coal min-

The North Staffordshire field was noted for its deep pits; many were well over 1,000ft deep, and Stafford Colliery, Fenton, was the deepest in the country at over 3,300ft.

But coal had its price, and not all coal mining ventures proved successful. Finding the coal in the first place could prove very difficult. On New Year's Day 1872, Major Arden cut the first sod of the Fair Oak Colliery near Rugeley. By 1875 the shaft was 811ft deep, sinking had proved difficult owing to flooding, and no coal had been struck. A second shaft was sunk, and coal was eventually found.

ing on a localized scale probably existed as early as the 12th century; in the south the earliest records date from the late 13th century. By the mid 17th century, mining operations in South Staffordshire were producing an estimated annual output of 50,000 tonnes; this was to rise dramatically once the county was linked to the fledgling canal network. The North Staffordshire coalfield would prove to be the most productive; by the beginning of the Second World War its output was more than the combined tonnage of the Cannock Chase and Black Country fields put together.

However, the workable reserve lasted only a few years; despite attempts to locate deeper measures, Fair Oak closed in July 1884 and the company went into liquidation. Flooding of the pits continued to prove a serious problem. In December 1872 the Cannock & Huntington Colliery Co began sinking Littleton Colliery, but the flooding was so serious that work was suspended in July 1881 without a single tonne of coal being raised. In 1897 Lord Hatherton formed a new company and work began again. The No 2 shaft reached a depth of 1,642ft in February 1899.

Finally, a third shaft was sunk in July 1900, but even so, it was not until November 1902 that coal was finally reached at a depth of 1,663ft.

Of course, the cost of coal, measured in human life, could be very great indeed. The county suffered its share of mining disasters, such as the one at the Minnie Pit, at Stoke-on-Trent. There, in January 1918, an explosion claimed 160 casualties.

Another great Staffordshire industry is brewing, which is centred on Burton upon Trent. Just when brewing started here is uncertain, though tradition says that it began during the 13th century when one of the abbots of Burton Abbey discovered that the local water was ideal for making beer of good quality. During her stay at Tutbury Castle, Mary, Queen of Scots swore by the stuff, and by the end of the 17th century, Burton Ale was on sale in London. Many of the breweries date from the 18th century. Benjamin Wilson had opened a brewery on the east side of the High Street by 1742, which was sold to Samuel Allsopp in 1807. Also in the High Street were the breweries of William Worthington (1760), William Bass (1777) and Thomas Salt (1807-12). In the 1870s Bass undertook a major expansion programme, building ale stores and cask-washing banks at Dixie, and a new maltings, bottling stores, ale stores and cask-washing facilities at Shobnall. At its height Bass' sites covered over 800 acres around Burton. In 1914 Worthingtons absorbed the Burton Brewery Co, and Worthington itself eventually merged with Bass, Ratcliffe & Gretton. Salts, who had a cooperage, maltings and stores in Anderstaff Lane, went into voluntary liquidation in May 1928. In 1934 Samuel Allsopp & Sons merged with Ind Coope, the latter having been established in

Station Street in 1856. Another 19th century newcomer was Phillips Brothers in Derby Street. They opened in 1865 on a prime site with excellent rail access, a fact not lost on Truman, Hanbury & Buxton, who took over the brewery in 1873. They spent a fortune on the place, extending the size of the operation and installing railway sidings throughout. The business survived for nearly one hundred years; it was acquired by Grand Metropolitan Hotels in August 1971, who then closed it down.

One last Staffordshire industry that hardly gets a mention is railway locomotive manufacturing. The county had, at one time or another, four firms building locomotives on a commercial basis, and two main line locomotive workshops. In Burton were the Baguley Cars and Thornewill & Wareham. Baguley started up in 1903 as the Rykneld Engine Co, changing its name in 1911. They built a few steam locomotives, but their main product range consisted of petrol and diesel locomotives mainly for industrial use; they also turned out units for the growing miniature railway and pleasure gardens market, and they built locomotives for the Drewery Car Co.

Thornewill & Wareham were iron and brass founders and millwrights who manufactured winding engines, boilers and steam driven plant. They began building railway locomotives during the late 1850s. The Burton breweries and the North Staffordshire collieries were amongst their customers. No one really knows how many locomotives were built by them before they gave it up around 1900.

Of the other firms, William Bagnall & Co, Castle Engine Works, Stafford, built several thousand steam locomotives and some diesels; these were mainly for industrial use in collieries, factories, steel works, quarries and other locations world wide. Kerr Stuart & Co, California Works, Stoke, again supplied markets world wide, including a number of locomotives for working sugar plantations. The main line workshops were the Great Western Railway at Stafford Road, Wolverhampton, and the North Staffordshire Railway shops at Stoke.

THE POTTERIES

◆◆

Of the six towns that make up the Potteries, Burslem and Fenton have a history going back to at least the 10th century, and along with Penkhill and Thurfield, they are mentioned in the Domesday Book. There is no mention of a village at Stoke, but there was certainly a church there in 1086. The parish of Stoke embraced a number of townships including: Burslem, Fenton, Hanley, Lane End, Newcastle, Norton-in-the-Moors and Whitmore.

Just how long pottery has been manufac-tured in the area is anyone's guess. The earliest examples date from around 1700BC, and excavations have established that quality pottery was being manufactured during the Roman occupation. The Romans would almost certainly have exported pottery made in Staffordshire to other parts of the province, and perhaps even to Gaul and Germania, but following the collapse of the Western Empire wares would have been produced for more local markets.

By the medieval period Burslem was developing as the most important township for the manufacture of pottery; the remains of two late 13th century kilns have been unearthed at Sneyd Green, and others are known to have existed. By the 16th century, Burslem was a centre for slip-ware; it was here that the butter pots for the important cheese and butter markets held at Uttoxeter were manufactured.

Though there was an abundant supply of coal, local supplies of clay were insufficient to meet the growing demand; potters were forced to import clay from Devon and

Cornwall. Josiah Wedgwood (1730-1795) was one of the prime movers for the building of the Trent & Mersey Canal. Staffordshire had no navigable rivers, and the canal offered pottery manufacturers an economy of scale which could not be matched by the packhorse trains. In 1766 the Trent & Mersey Act was passed by Parliament, authorizing the building of a navigation route from the River Trent to a junction with a proposed extension of the Bridgewater Canal at Runcorn Gap. On 26 July that same year, Josiah cut the first sod. The canal opened in 1777, complete with the engineer James Brindley's masterpiece - the 2,900yd tunnel under Harecastle Hill.

The canal was an immediate success. Flint and china clay could now be trans-shipped at Runcorn for direct delivery to the factories around Burslem, and finished products could be sent in bulk to Liverpool and Hull. The importance of the canal in stimulating the pottery industry cannot be underestimated. Not only did it give the Potteries the opportunity to provide wares for overseas markets, but its connections with no less than eight other canal systems, or significant branches, meant that most of England could be supplied.

A TALE OF OLD CANNOCK CHASE

Cannock Chase was once so thickly wooded that it was said that strangers would soon lose their way unless accompanied by someone who knew the route. It was also bandit country, but not all the bandits were from the bottom rung of society's ladder. In 1342 some merchants in Lichfield dispatched a couple of servants and packhorses with goods to sell at the next Stafford market. They were intercepted 'beneath Cannock Wood' by Sir Robert de Ridware and two squires. Ridware seized the servants and the goods and headed off to the priory at Lapley. On the way, one of the servants gave Ridware the slip, returned to Lichfield and called out the sheriff. In the meantime, Ridware had reached the priory where he met up with several other knights who also seem to have been engaged in a little freelance robbery. The knights then shared out their spoils and went their separate ways. It was near Blythebury that the sheriff of Lichfield caught up with Ridware. Some goods were recovered, and four of Ridware's men were hanged on the spot. Not to be outdone, Sir Robert rode to his kinsman Walter de Ridware, Lord of Hamstall Ridware, and asked for help. Walter provided Sir Robert with enough men for him to attack the sheriff's party and retake the stolen goods. The merchants later made their way to Stafford to plead their case, but found Ridware's men at the very gates of the town. The merchants are said to have come close to being assaulted by Ridware's men and only just escaped.

BIDDULPH, HIGH STREET c1955 B611015

At this time boys were often in their teens before they got a pair of long trousers. Jeans were unheard of, and the design of children's clothes had hardly changed for thirty years. The three boys on the left could have stepped straight out of the late 1920s. Jeans did not become readily available until around 1960, when they could be bought for as little as 7s 6d a pair.

BIDDULPH, THE GRANGE 1902 48668

Biddulph Grange stands amid the magnificent gardens laid out by one of the great 19th century horticulturists, James Bateman. Bateman was also responsible for laying out the Arboretum at Derby, the first public park in England. The Grange later became a children's hospital.

BIDDULPH
High Street and War Memorial c1955 B611014
In an earlier conflict John Bowyer, who was baptized at
Biddulph in 1623, raised a company of foot for the
Parliamentary army, and served with distinction at Hopton
Heath. He was later appointed Governor of Leek and
authorized to raise two Troops of Horse and to bring his
company up to full regimental strength.

BIDDULPH, MOW COP CASTLE c1955 B611028

BIDDULPH
Mow Cop Castle c1955
Mow Cop could be said to be the birthplace of the Primitive Methodist movement, for it was here in 1807 that Hugh Bourne (1772-1852) and William Clowes (1780-1851) held their first meetings. Expelled by the Methodist Conference, the men continued to preach and in 1811 adopted the name Primitive Methodists.

◆

KIDSGROVE
Liverpool Road c1955
Kidsgrove is situated within the North Staffordshire coal field, and it was at a mine in the area in 1837 that deep mining was being carried out at 975ft below the surface. The deepest mine at this time, however, was at Apedale, where men were working at depths in excess of 2,000ft.

KIDSGROVE, LIVERPOOL ROAD c1955 K145004

KIDSGROVE, THE SHOPPING CENTRE c1965 K145040

This was in the days when supermarkets complemented high street shopping. Out of town shopping and subsequently deserted high streets were still some way off in the future.

TUNSTALL, HIGH STREET c1955 T88014

One hundred years before this, there were no large shops in the town, and the age of the department store was still a few years away. If you needed to buy a pair of boots in 1855, the local shoemaker would have perhaps fifteen or so pairs for show. From these you would select a design and they would then be made to order. The nearest place where ready-made boots could be bought was Burslem.

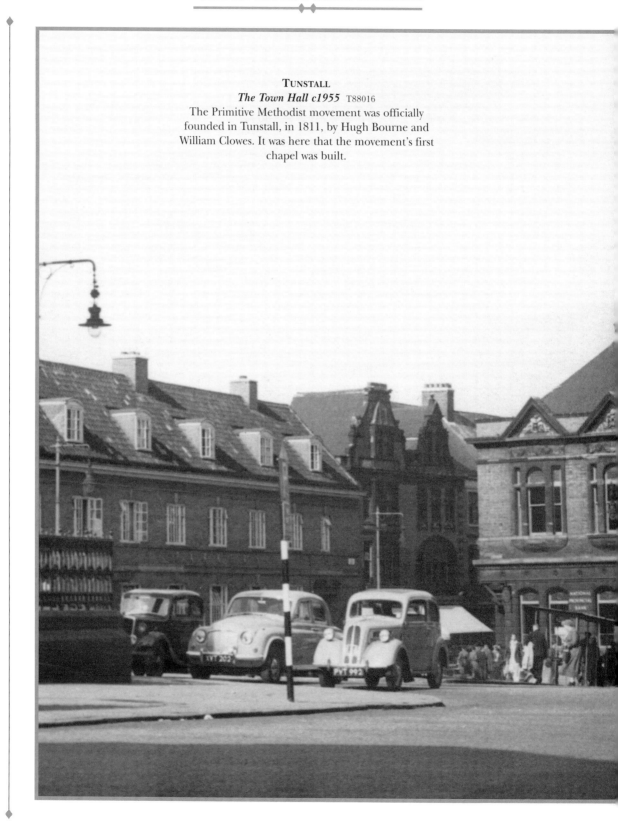

TUNSTALL
The Town Hall c1955 T88016
The Primitive Methodist movement was officially
founded in Tunstall, in 1811, by Hugh Bourne and
William Clowes. It was here that the movement's first
chapel was built.

TUNSTALL, THE SQUARE 1940 T88003

About a hundred years before this picture was taken, Tunstall market was always busiest on Saturday evenings, and like the one at Crewe probably stayed open until 10pm. It was cheaper to shop in Tunstall than to go to Hanley by road, as there were three toll booths to get through.

TUNSTALL, THE TOWN HALL 1940 T88001

In the early-1850s, an old soldier lived in Tunstall who, because he was a veteran of Wellington's army at Waterloo, went by the name of 'Waterloo'. His claim to fame was that one of his arms was a mass of warts from elbow to fingertips, the only clear bit being the palm of his hand. Waterloo sold his arm to a local doctor for an advance payment of half a guinea, the arm to be removed on his death.

BURSLEM, GENERAL VIEW 1956 B303002
Bottle kilns were once a familiar sight throughout the Potteries, and there were about 2,000 of them in the late 1930s. Later, they fell victim both to progress and anti-pollution legislation, and were replaced by gas-fired and electric kilns. The last bottle kiln to be used commercially closed down in 1967.

BURSLEM, GENERAL VIEW 1956 B303003
The industrial landscape of Burslem was dominated by bottle kilns and slag heaps. At this time, the Staffordshire potteries were employing about 60,000 workers. The North Staffordshire area of the National Coal Board included such collieries as Chatterley Whitfield, Norton & Biddulph, Silverdale, Wolstanton, and Trentham.

HANLEY, THE TOWN CENTRE c1965 H334002

Dating only from 1737, Hanley was a township in the parish of Stoke until 1857. It is now the principal shopping centre for the surrounding area, enhanced by recent one-way traffic systems and pedestrian schemes. It is also here that Stoke-on-Trent's world-famous collection of Staffordshire figures, pottery, porcelain and ceramics are housed in a superb museum.

HANLEY, FOUNTAIN SQUARE c1965 H334009

Hanley has two famous sons: the author Arnold Bennett and the aircraft designer Reginald Mitchell were both born in the town. Bennett is renowned for his novels based on The Potteries, and Mitchell was the designer of the legendary Spitfire fighter.

NEWCASTLE-UNDER-LYME
High Street c1965
The Royalists had a verse about local lad
and Parliamentary general, Thomas
Harrison: 'Son of a witch, Mayest thou
die in a ditch, With the butchers who
back up thy quarrels, And art above
ground, While the world shall resound,
A welcome to Royal King Charles'.

◆

NEWCASTLE-UNDER-LYME
High Street c1940
Major-general Thomas Harrison, who
served in the Parliamentary army during
the Civil War, was born in a house on the
High Street. His father, grandfather, and
great grandfather were all butchers, and
held various council offices. Between
1552 and 1565, grandfather Richard was
a councillor, but was also at different
times constable, sergeant and bailiff.

NEWCASTLE-UNDER-LYME, HIGH STREET C1965 N93025

NEWCASTLE-UNDER-LYME, HIGH STREET C1940 N93005

NEWCASTLE-UNDER-LYME
High Street c1955   N93016

The Guildhall is the town's oldest public building, dating from about 1714, but it was heavily restored during the mid 19th century. By the beginning of the 17th century those Englishmen who could afford it had taken up the craze for smoking tobacco in pipes made of clay. Newcastle's pipemakers gained a reputation for turning out quality pipes, for the clays between Shelton and Hanley Green were particularly suitable.

NEWCASTLE-UNDER-LYME, HIGH STREET 1965 N93049

When this picture of the High Street was taken, there would be plenty of outlets from which it was possible to buy tobacco products. Not so in 1633, when there were only three licensed sellers in the whole town: grocers Philip Sherwin (who later became mayor) and Thomas Hunt, and the apothecary John Stubbs.

NEWCASTLE-UNDER-LYME, THE TOWN CENTRE c1965 N93046

The wide end of the Ironmarket was also known as Butchers' Row; even its supply of water came to the surface courtesy of the Butchery Pump. Also here was the Iron Hall which belonged to the castle chapel of St Mary, from which it drew rents. In 1608 Thomas Baylie, a butcher, was paying an annual rent of 12d for a tenement in the Iron Hall.

TRENTHAM, THE HALL 1900 46211

Trentham Hall, from the southwest. Originally built in the early 17th century by Sir Richard Leveson, it was extended by his descendants and rebuilt in the Italianate style between 1834 and 1844 to designs by Charles Barry.

TRENTHAM, THE HALL 1900 46213

At this time Trentham Hall was still used by the Dukes of Sutherland, and local people were allowed access to the gardens on public holidays and during Wakes Week. Within a few years, however, the Sutherlands had abandoned Trentham: in 1910 the fourth Duke offered it for sale to the county borough of Stoke-on-Trent. When his offer was declined, the duke had many of the buildings dismantled and the stone sold off. Today Trentham is a leading conference, exhibition, function and leisure centre.

SWYNNERTON
THE VILLAGE 1900 46206

Swynnerton lies about three miles south of Trentham. It was Roger de Swinnerton, Lord of the Manor, who obtained a charter from Edward I to hold a market here every Wednesday and an annual fair on the feast day of Our Lady's assumption. The manor later passed into the hands of the Fitzherbert family, and the church was once under the patronage of Oxford University.

LEEK
The Market Place c1955 L379007

Leek was settled before the Roman occupation, the name deriving from 'Llech', a stone. Standing as it does at the southern end of some of the most spectacular scenery in the midlands, the area has been popular with tourists for nearly two hundred years. Tourism was given a boost in the 1840s when the North Staffordshire Railway opened its line through the Churnet Valley.

LEEK, THE MARKET PLACE c1955 L379003

The stall holders and the ice cream man must be wondering where the customers are. They must either all be at work, or down at Rudyard Lake for the day. By the mid-1950s, Leek had become a major centre for the knitwear industry: three-quarters of all the scarves worn in the UK were said to have been manufactured in the town.

LEEK, DERBY STREET c1955 L379004

There are two interesting churches in Leek. All Saints Church dates from the 1880s and is decorated in the Arts and Crafts style, with glass by Morris & Co. The parish church, dedicated to St Edward the Confessor, is mainly 14th century, though the chancel was rebuilt during the 19th century.

LEEK, ST EDWARD'S STREET c1955 L379009

The parish church is at the top of the street, out of camera shot. This is also an area of the town known as Petty France because, along with Ashbourne in Derbyshire, Leek was used to house French prisoners during the Napoleonic Wars.

ALSTONEFIELD, MILL DALE c1955 A284002

Alstonefield is situated in the valley of the Dove, four miles east of Leek. It has a larger number of pre-Norman carved stones than anywhere else in the county. The parish church of St Peter features a Norman south door and chancel arch, and the Cotton family pew. Charles Cotton was Isaac Walton's friend, and the pair often sat together in church.

ALTON TOWERS C1955 A216169

ALTON TOWERS
c1955

In 1831 John, Earl of Shrewsbury, made this house his permanent home. In the late 1860s the then Earl hired John Mason Cook, son of pioneer travel agent, Thomas Cook, to promote the gardens at Alton Towers. Cook's first excursion to Alton resulted in a staggering 10,000 visitors in one day.

◆

ALTON TOWERS
The Lake and Hall c1955

The estate was sold in 1924 to a private company, who opened it to the public. During the Second World War it was used as an officer training unit, but when peace came it was allowed to stand empty and neglected for about six years, leaving much of the building a ruin. Today Alton is one of the country's leading tourist attractions.

ALTON TOWERS, THE LAKE AND HALL C1955 A216171

ALTON, LOWER VILLAGE c1955 A285008

When W H N Nithersdale wrote his book on the Highlands of Staffordshire, he was impressed by the number of public houses in the village, all of which did a roaring trade during the summer months and at weekends. He should know: he was an inspector for the Inland Revenue.

ALTON, THE ROUND HOUSE c1955 A285006

The windowless stone-built village lock-up. A surprising number of these old roundhouse lock-ups survive, many in the villages of neighbouring Derbyshire. Even before the Great War business had been transferred to a 'much more commodious police station'.

ALTON, THE MILL CAFE AND CASTLE c1955 A285011
Perched high on its hill, Alton Castle dominates the area. It was rebuilt in the 15th century, then badly damaged during the Civil War, and rebuilt again. The castle was never a main residence for the Talbot family, though the sixteenth Earl commissioned Pugin to rebuild the place. The remains of the old castle are in the grounds.

ALTON, THE CASTLE C1955 A285001

At this time the Castle was being used as a Catholic preparatory school for boys. The original castle is thought to have been built by Bertram de Verdun, who also founded the Cistercian abbey at Croxden. Eventually in 1407 it passed by marriage to John Talbot, after being in the possession of the Furnivalle family for about one hundred years.

UTTOXETER, HIGH STREET C1955 U29040

It is said that no other town has such a choice in the way its name is pronounced: 'Ucheter', 'Uxeter', 'Toxeter', 'Itcheter', to name but four. In the Domesday Book Uttoxeter appears as Wotocheshede; by 1175 it was being called Uttokishedere, by 1242 Uittokesather, and by 1251 Huttokesather. Within a few more years it had been changed again, this time to Huttokeshagh.

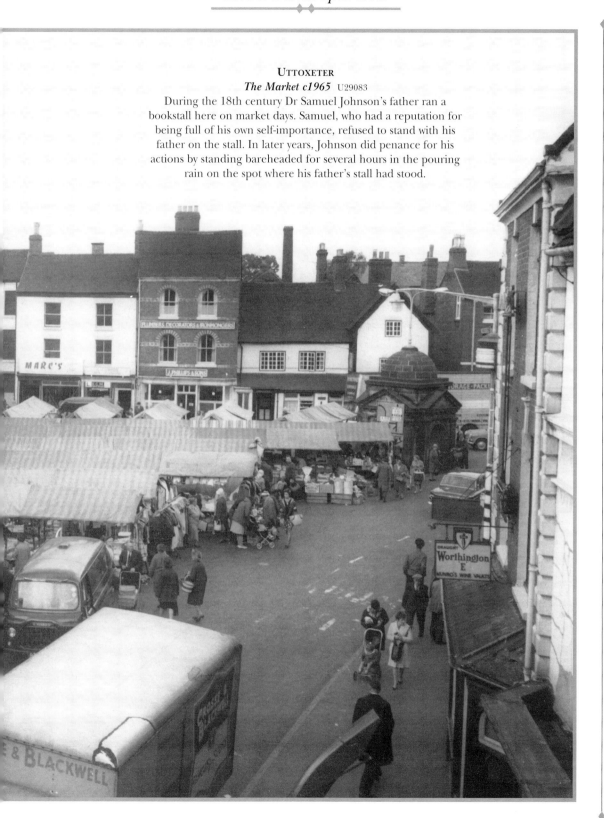

UTTOXETER

The Market c1965 U29083

During the 18th century Dr Samuel Johnson's father ran a
bookstall here on market days. Samuel, who had a reputation for
being full of his own self-importance, refused to stand with his
father on the stall. In later years, Johnson did penance for his
actions by standing bareheaded for several hours in the pouring
rain on the spot where his father's stall had stood.

UTTOXETER, THE MARKET PLACE c1955 U29012

In the late 17th century the town had an established, high-quality cheese and butter market, with buyers coming from as far as London to do business. One of the ways farmers cheated their customers was to fill only the top portion of the 14lb butter jars and leave the remainder empty. Counter-measures included an instrument rather like an overgrown cheese taster, long enough to reach the bottom of the jar and take a core sample.

UTTOXETER, THE HOCKLEY c1955 U29037

During the Civil War, Sir John Gell was asked by Staffordshire moorlanders for help against the Royalist garrison at Stafford. With the promise of a large contingent of moorlanders, Gell moved his force, which included artillery, to Uttoxeter. Few moorlanders turned up. Gell took a look at Stafford but considered the garrison too strong, so he withdrew to Derby.

UTTOXETER, THE CATTLE MARKET c1965 U29077

From the 12th century, the rearing of sheep for their wool became a major source of revenue for the monastic houses in the north of England. The largest producer in the county was Croxden Abbey with at least 7,000 sheep. Burton Abbey had around 6,000 and Dieulacres Abbey about 5,000. These flocks were, however, insignificant when set against those of the great Yorkshire monasteries of Fountains, Rievaulx and Kirkstall.

TUTBURY, THE CASTLE c1955 T165006

Built on a natural defensive site that had been used since the Bronze Age, Tutbury was garrisoned by Royalist troops during the Civil War. On 6 July 1644, Sir John Gell led his Parliamentarian force on a lightning raid, but was unable to take the fortress. Tutbury held out until April 1646, when it was forced to surrender due to an outbreak of the plague.

BURTON UPON TRENT, STATION ROAD 1961 B286015

The railway came to Burton in 1839 with the opening of the Birmingham & Derby Junction. One immediate effect was that the railways provided the breweries with a golden opportunity to reach more outlets and sell more beer. In the 1960s Burton was notorious for the number of level crossings that existed in and around the town on the brewery railway system.

BURTON UPON TRENT, THE TOWN HALL c1965 B286069

The Town Hall was given to Burton by Michael Bass, who also financed the building of St Paul's and St Margaret's churches. Brewing on a commercial scale was introduced by Benjamin Wilson in the mid 18th century. William Bass opened his brewery in the High Street in 1777. By 1796 there were nine breweries in the town.

BURTON UPON TRENT, THE BRIDGE c1965 B286020

Burton Bridge was once one of only a handful of crossing points over the Trent River, and consequently the town was of some strategic importance. In 1322 Thomas, Earl of Lancaster, rebelled against the authority of Edward II and occupied the bridge. However, the King's troops forced their way across and the Earl fled, but not before setting fire to the town.

BURTON UPON TRENT, HIGH STREET 1961 B286017

The parish church is dedicated to St Modwen, the founder of a 7th century Christian settlement at Burton. The first monastic house in the county was founded at Burton, endowed by the Saxon thegn, Wulfric Spot. The Benedictine abbey survived until the Dissolution, when its lands were acquired by Sir William Paget.

BURTON UPON TRENT, FERRY BRIDGE c1965 B286006

The River Trent at Burton is now crossed by three bridges: Burton Bridge, built in 1864, the iron Angelsey Bridge and the Stapenhill Viaduct, which is in fact a footbridge.

BRANSTON, SUTHERLAND JUNIOR AND INFANTS SCHOOL c1955 B747002
The pupils of the school line the railings looking at the man with the camera. Branston is just two miles south of Burton, and at one time belonged to Burton Abbey. It was made a parish in its own right in 1870.

BARTON-UNDER-NEEDWOOD, THE VILLAGE c1955 B527004
The village gets its name from a Barton (or Berton), the old word for a rickyard. The village church of St James was remarkable for its time in that it was built all at once, and not over a couple of centuries. It was paid for by Dr John Taylor, a man of humble origins who rose through the ranks to become chaplain to Henry VIII and Master of the Rolls. The church was built in 1533.

ABBOTS BROMLEY
The Horn Dance c1955 A165385
Every year, on the first Monday after the Sunday
following 4 September, the Horn Dance is
performed in Abbots Bromley. No one knows how
old the dance is; it could easily predate the
Norman Conquest, and its meaning is also lost to
us. Ten dancers take part accompanied by two
musicians. The dancers include a maid
(Maid Marian), a jester, a man on a hobby-horse,
a boy with a bow and arrow and six
men wearing antlers.

ABBOTS BROMLEY, THE MARKET PLACE c1955 A165003
There are quite a few old, half-timbered buildings still extant in the village, but perhaps the most interesting is the old market house, which can be seen on the left of the picture. It is not the half-timbered building, but the open-sided structure.

STONE, VIEW FROM THE BREWERY 1900 46169
The view from the roof of Bent's Brewery. In the 12th century there was an Augustinian priory in the village. Suppressed during the Dissolution, the monastic church, which was also the parish church, survived. Of the priory, however, little remained even in 1900, save for the remains of the cloisters and a stone arch.

STONE, HIGH STREET 1900 46170
The Manor of Stone was not mentioned in the Domesday Book, though it was given by William the Conqueror to one Erasmus de Walton. His family held it until the reign of Henry I. Later, the manor became forfeit to the Crown, because Enysan de Walton killed two nuns and a priest.

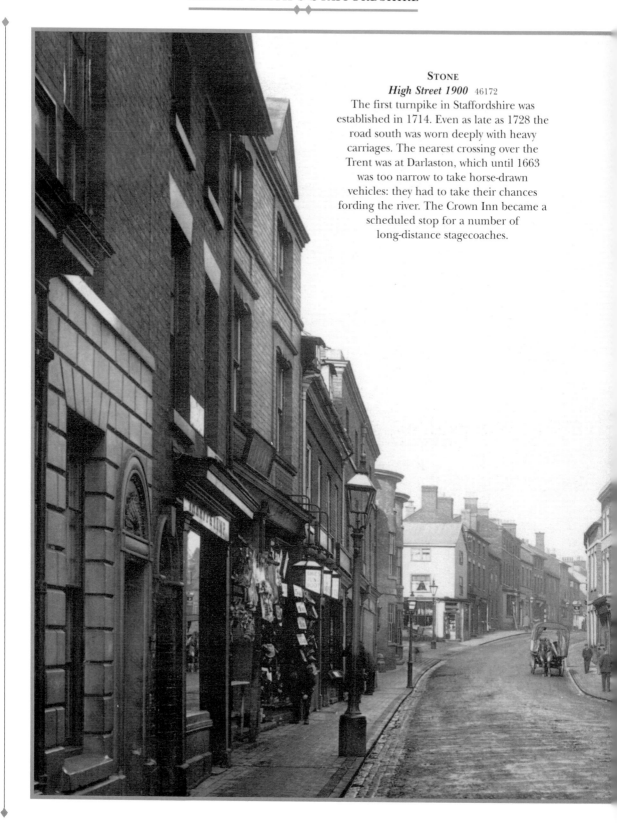

STONE
High Street 1900 46172
The first turnpike in Staffordshire was established in 1714. Even as late as 1728 the road south was worn deeply with heavy carriages. The nearest crossing over the Trent was at Darlaston, which until 1663 was too narrow to take horse-drawn vehicles: they had to take their chances fording the river. The Crown Inn became a scheduled stop for a number of long-distance stagecoaches.

STONE, HIGH STREET 1900 46171

The town grew up astride what was the most important road in medieval England, that between London and Chester, at that time the principal port for Ireland. The old parish included the townships of Beech, Kibblestone, Hilderstone and Normacott, and in 1811 the population was around 6,000 people.

STONE, GRANVILLE SQUARE 1900 46173

How did Stone get its name? One story is that it is derived from a cairn erected over the bodies of the two sons of Wulfhere, a 7th century King of Mercia who slew his sons because they had adopted Christianity and been baptized by St Chad. Then, full of remorse for what he had done, Wulfhere founded a monastery at Stone and adopted Christianity himself.

STONE, BENTS BREWERY 1900 46189

Other than Burton, brewing in Staffordshire received a shot in the arm with the opening in 1992 of the Lichfield Brewery, which produces such delights as Resurrection Ale and Xpired. Other independent breweries include The Rising Sun Inn, Audley; the Stony Rock Brewery, Waterhouses; and the Titanic Brewery, Burslem.

STONE, THE RAILWAY STATION 1900 46175

The elegant exterior of the station, which belonged to the North Staffordshire Railway Co. Stone was on the North Staffordshire line from Stoke, which linked with the London & North Western at Colwick West Junction. There was also a connecting line from Stone to Norton Bridge, on the LNWR route between Crewe and Stafford. Stone closed to goods traffic in 1967.

ECCLESHALL

High Street 1900 46156

By the beginning of the 11th century the parish was doing well enough to support five churches and two chapels. Then disaster struck. In 1010 Danish raiders attacked and all but destroyed the place. Eccleshall itself was left in ruins. It was not until 1090 that the old church was rebuilt and dedicated to Holy Trinity. The town looks prosperous enough in this photograph.

ECCLESHALL, HIGH STREET 1900 46157

This small market town on the banks of the Sow was entitled to hold four annual fairs, mainly for the buying and selling of horses and cattle. They were held on Midlent Thursday, Holy Thursday, 5 August, and the first Friday in November. A regular weekly market was held every Friday.

ECCLESHALL, HIGH STREET 1900 46158

The village features in the story surrounding Wulfhere of Mercia and his two sons Ulfred and Rufin. The two claimed to be going hunting, but came instead to Eccleshall; here they were baptized by Bishop Chad. Wulfhere caught his sons praying, and in a fit of rage killed them and then destroyed the church. He is then said to have repented, converted to Christianity, and rebuilt the church.

ECCLESHALL
The Castle c1965

In 1209, the rebuilding of Eccleshall Castle was begun by Walter Langton, Bishop of Lichfield and Lord High Treasurer of England. During the Civil War it was garrisoned by Royalist troops, but fell in August 1643 after an eight-week siege. In 1695 Bishop Lloyd began rebuilding the castle, and it continued as a residence until the death of Bishop Lonsdale in 1867.

◆

ECCLESHALL
Stafford Street 1900

By 1920 the King's Arms was RAC and ACU (Auto Cycle Union) listed. It offered garaging for automobiles, but anyone intending to stay at the King's Arms had to either to send a wire or turn up on spec, as there was no telephone.

ECCLESHALL, THE CASTLE c1965 E18023

ECCLESHALL, STAFFORD STREET 1900 46159

STAFFORD, ANCIENT HIGH HOUSE 1948 S411010
Stafford's oldest house is the four-storey, half-timbered High House, which dates from around 1555. It was here that King Charles and Prince Rupert had their quarters during the King's march from Derby to Shrewsbury in September 1642. On 11 September, Rupert had led an assault on Caldecote House, the defenders put up a stiff resistance. On finding that the garrison consisted of six women and three men, the Prince ordered his troops to withdraw.

STAFFORD, GAOLGATE STREET c1955 S411021

Stafford has two interesting churches. The Church of St Mary has an unusual octagonal tower: it was here that Isaac Walton was baptized in 1593. The other church, St Chad's, was said to be almost derelict by 1650. However, restoration work was carried out between 1854 and 1875, saving the Norman nave and chancel arch. The Norman-style font actually dates from 1856 and the reredos from 1910.

STAFFORD, THE CASTLE c1955 S411002

The first castle on this site is thought to have been built by Robert de Stafford during the 1070s. The timber keep was replaced by one built of stone, and about 1350 the fortress underwent extensive rebuilding. During the Civil War the castle was ably defended by the Dowager Lady Stafford, but after it had fallen, it was slighted. In the early 19th century rebuilding began, but the project was abandoned before completion.

STAFFORD
The Royal Baths c1955 S411004
During the 19th century the borough council were desperately seeking new fresh water supplies for the town. Bore holes were sunk, and during one of these operations salt was struck at a depth of 400 ft. Bathing in brine was all the rage in Victorian England; casks of salt were shipped daily from Nantwich to people's homes. The Royal Brine Baths were opened in 1892.

PENKRIDGE, MAIN ROAD 1963 P129001

PENKRIDGE
Main Road 1963
Penkridge was important in Saxon times, and in 958 Edgar of Mercia dated a charter from 'the famous place, which is called Penric'. The parish church was one of the six collegiate churches of Staffordshire. Nearby is Pillaton Hall, the home of the Littleton family for three centuries.

◆

RUGELEY
Market Square c1955
Industry came early to Rugeley. There was a forge in the area by 1273, and glassmaking was well established by the early 14th century. John Glasman supplied stained glass for the East Window of York Minster. The earliest slitting mill in the midlands is thought to have opened at Rugeley in 1623.

RUGELEY, MARKET SQUARE c1955 R271006

RUGELEY, THE MARKET PLACE 1951 R271004
The only mention that Rugeley gets in the 1920 Dunlop Book is for the twelve-bed Shrewsbury Arms, which could also provide garaging for eight automobiles.

RUGELEY, LOWER BROOK STREET c1955 R271023
In 1954 the NCB sank its first pit in the country at Lea Hall, Rugeley. The colliery opened in July 1960; most of its output went by conveyor direct to nearby Rugeley, a power station. Lea Hall closed in December 1990.

CANNOCK, GENERAL VIEW c1955 C339301
There are few old buildings surviving in the town. St Luke's Church dates from the 12th century, but little remains of the original. Cannock does, however, possess one of the finest bowling greens in the country, which has been in use for nearly two hundred years.

CANNOCK, THE SQUARE c1965 C339092
Trees shade the broad square. The street is a pleasing mix of Victorian shops and modern infill.

CANNOCK, THE MARKET PLACE c1965 C339173

Between 1801 and 1901 the industrialisation process brought tens of thousands of people into Staffordshire. The population of Cannock rose from 1,359 to 23,974; Wolverhampton from 12,565 to 94,187. During the same period many rural places saw either a gradual increase or loss in population. Eccleshall went up from 3,734 to 4,186 but Gnosall fell from 2,246 to 2,085.

CANNOCK, THE TOWN CENTRE c1955 C339030

There was a time when Cannock had pretensions to being a spa town, as did many others; Robert Plot, in 'The Natural History of Staffordshire '(1686), records nineteen mineral springs in the county. These springs were old holy wells. For every town that made it as a spa, ten failed. Cannock didn't make it.

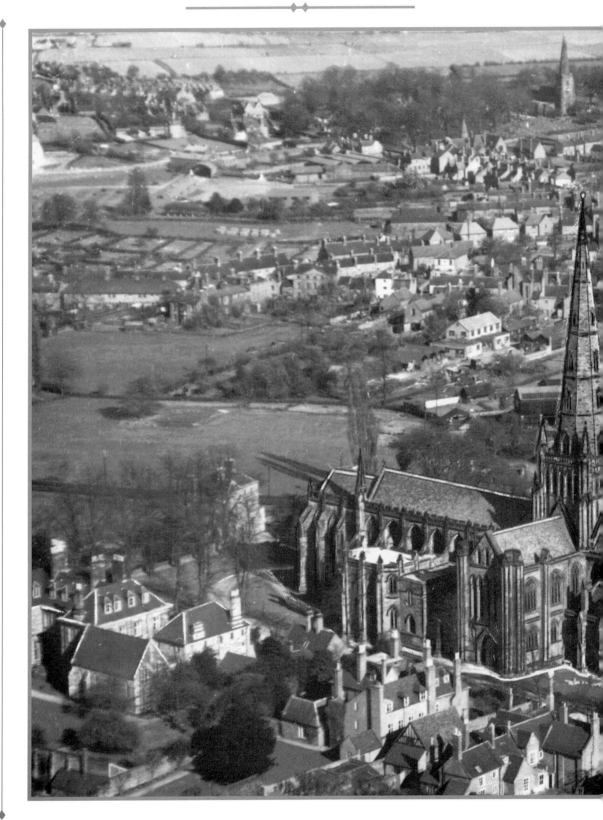

LICHFIELD
The Cathedral c1955 L45052
An excellent aerial view of the Cathedral. Work on the
present structure began in the late 12th century, and took
around 150 years to complete, though
additional work was undertaken during the 15th century.
The cathedral was badly damaged during the Civil War: the
central spire was all but destroyed, and much of the building
was left roofless.

LICHFIELD, THE CATHEDRAL 1887 20222

During the Civil War the cathedral and its surrounding Close were fortified and held for the King; the rest of the city declared for Parliament. Parliamentarian troops under Lord Brooke attacked. Brooke prayed publicly that 'if the cause he were in were not right and just, he might be presently cut off'. He was shot dead later that day. The garrison surrendered three days later, and were allowed to leave.

LICHFIELD, BIRD STREET c1955 L45055

On the right is the Swan, the only hotel in the city in the 1920s to be RAC and AA listed. The city's other leading hotel, the George, was once the main coaching inn and is also the setting for George Farquhar's (1678-1707) 'Beaux' Stratagem'. At the beginning of the 20th century, both hotels charged the same rates: 4s a night for a room and 2s 6d for dinner.

LICHFIELD, DR JOHNSON'S STATUE c1955 L45008

Dr Johnson's statue in the Market Square was erected in 1838, and has bas-reliefs relating to scenes from his life on the pedestal. He was born in Breadmarket Street, where his father ran a bookshop. Every year on the Saturday nearest Johnson's birthday, there is an official gathering around his statue, followed by a supper in the Guildhall.

LICHFIELD, MARKET SQUARE c1955 L45034
At the other end of the Market Square is the bronze statue of James Boswell, drinking companion and biographer of Samuel Johnson. His statue was not erected until 1908. Also at this end is a memorial to Edward Wightman, the last man in England to be burnt at the stake for heresy.

TAMWORTH, THE CASTLE c1960 T157015
Soon after the Conquest, the Normans built a wooden motte and bailey castle at Tamworth on the site of the Mercian fortifications of 913. This was replaced by the shell-keep and tower, which still stand. By the mid 16th century much of the castle was in ruins, though some construction work was done at this time, including the superb banqueting hall. The castle was sold to the corporation in 1897 by the 5th Marquess of Townsend.

TAMWORTH, THE TOWN HALL c1955 T157001

The Town Hall was built in 1701 by Thomas Guy, the local MP. The building is noted for its high-pitched roof, Jacobean windows and cupola. Tamworth fails to get a mention in the Domesday Book, but this is believed to be due to a clerical error caused by the fact that the town straddles the border between Staffordshire and Warwickshire. London is another place not covered by Domesday.

TAMWORTH, GENERAL VIEW c1965 T157060

A unique feature of the parish church, dedicated to St Editha, is the tower. Topped-off with small spires at each corner, it also has a double spiral staircase. The staircases are designed in such a way that the floor of one is the roof of the other, and people using them do not see one another until they reach the top of the tower.

TAMWORTH, GEORGE STREET c1955 T157004

Even the close proximity of several coal mines did not cause Tamworth to lose its market town image. After the Great War the town was still quite small, with a population of about 7,700, making it smaller than Lichfield (8,600); Aberystwyth (8,400); Bideford (9,000) and Melton Mowbray (9,200).

TAMWORTH
Silver Street 1949

A charter of 1560 appeared to give the vote to the 'commonality' of the town. In 1669 Lord Clifford secured the vote of the council, but John Ferrers won because the common people had voted for him. After Parliament's concern about anarchy from giving votes 'to the great unwashed' Ferrers lost his seat.

◆

HOPWAS
The Canal c1955

The Birmingham & Fazerley Canal, completed in 1789, provided a more direct route for London-bound goods. It was a unique example of co-operation between canal companies. The Coventry Canal agreed to extend northwards from Atherstone to Fazerley, whilst the B&F undertook to complete the proposed section from Fazerley to Whittington.

TAMWORTH, SILVER STREET 1949 T157009

HOPWAS, THE CANAL c1955 H413002

DRAYTON BASSETT, THE GREEN c1965 D192006

The B & F route also relied on the Oxford Canal, agreeing to complete its route to the Thames if Grand Trunk built the Coventry section from Whittington to Fradley. The problem with the Coventry Canal Co was that by 1771 they had only completed as far as Atherstone when the money ran out. Drayton Bassett is situated four miles south of Tamworth.

DRAYTON BASSETT, THE CANAL AND SWING BRIDGE c1965 D192002

The canal at Drayton Manor, with its unique Gothic-style footbridge, complete with battlements. Immediately beyond is a swing bridge. The 15-acre Drayton Manor park and zoo is close by; the village of Drayton Bassett is to the southwest.

BREWOOD
The Canal and Bridge c1965

In 1846 the Shropshire Union Canal Co was formed by the amalgamation of several companies. The main canal ran from Whitby, now Ellesmere Port on the Mersey, to Autherley near Wolverhampton, through 46 sets of locks. Brewood is situated five miles along the canal from its junction with the Staffordshire & Worcestershire.

BREWOOD
Dean Street c1965

The 13th-century church contains monuments to the Giffard family. A devout Catholic, Sir John Giffard was hauled before the Privy Council to answer charges of not conforming to the established church, just three days after lavishly entertaining Queen Elizabeth I at Chillington Hall.

BREWOOD, THE CANAL AND BRIDGE c1965 B680002

BREWOOD, DEAN STREET c1965 B680010

WHEATON ASTON, THE LOCK c1955 W286001

From here the canal maintains a level for over twenty miles until it reaches Tyrley, where a flight of five locks alter the level by 33 ft. At Tyrley the lock keeper's single storey cottage is situated between Locks 1 and 2. From Tyrley the canal crosses the Tern by a single-arched aqueduct and crosses the border into Shropshire.

WHEATON ASTON, THE GREEN c1955 W286006

Around this time Staffordshire dairy farms were producing nearly 80 million gallons of milk a year; by the 1960s it had risen to over 90 million gallons.

GNOSALL, THE WHARF AND TUNNEL c1955 G22304

Work on the canal at Gnosall began in 1830. One of the main problems facing the engineers was that they would have to bore a 690yd tunnel at Cowley. However, the rock they were boring through kept crumbling away, leaving the engineer in charge, William Povis, little choice but to open it out and take the top off. In the end, the tunnel, which can be seen in the distance, was reduced in length to just over eighty yards.

GNOSALL, THE VILLAGE 1899 44334

At this time only some 10 per cent of the county's agricultural land was in the hands of owner-occupiers; the majority was still controlled by the great estates. However, owners such as the 1st Lord Hatterton were at the forefront of agricultural development and improvement. Lord Hatterton even supported an agricultural school for the benefit of boys aged 10 to 14 years.

GNOSALL, THE VILLAGE 1899 44332
In the distance is the tower of the parish church, St Lawrence. Dating back to Norman times it was one of a number of collegiate churches established in the county; others included Penkridge, Tamworth and Wolverhampton. These churches enjoyed special status. They were founded on royal patronage and were exempt from the bishop's authority. However, Gnosall never achieved full collegiate status.

GNOSALL, THE VILLAGE 1899 44333
Most villages supported several shops and pubs. Gnosall also had two canal-side pubs, the Boat Inn by Bridge No 34, and the Navigation Inn by Bridge No 35.

KINVER, HIGH STREET c1965 K37104
Opened throughout in 1772, the Staffs & Worcestershire Canal was designed by James Brindley as part of a scheme to allow traffic to operate between the Thames, Trent, Severn and Mersey. At ten miles from Stourport, Kinver lies just to the west of Kinver Lock. The total length of the canal was just over 46 miles with 43 locks: it ran from the River Severn, at Stourport, to a junction with the Trent & Mersey, at Great Haywood.

KINVER
High Street 1931 84702
In the 1660s Kinver was the scene of an unsuccessful
attempt by Andrew Yarranton to make the Warwickshire
Stour navigable from Stourbridge to Stourport-on-Severn.
A cut was made across the outskirts of Kinver parish, which
can still be seen to this day. The river between
Kidderminster and Stourbridge did open for traffic, and
proved useful for the transportation of coals.

KINVER, HIGH STREET c1955 K37073

Kinver Forest once extended into Worcestershire. In Norman England forests were areas reserved for hunting. They had their own laws and courts and were policed by foresters. At Kinver a royal hunting lodge was in existence before 1100, though one was later built at Stourton. Around 1223 Stourton Lodge was fortified and later became known as Stourton Castle.

KINVER, HIGH STREET 1931 84701

In 1627 Richard Foley opened a slitting mill at Hyde in Kinver for the purpose of cutting iron rods into suitable lengths for nailers. At this time nailmaking was an important industry in southern Staffordshire. Within seven years Foley had established something of an industrial empire, operating a number of forges and furnaces, and claiming that he provided work for 800 people.

WOMBOURN
Bratch Locks c1965

The delightful whitewashed parapets and the octagonal toll-house of the Bratch Locks. Nearby are the waterworks opened by Bilston's urban district council in 1896. The main building is complete with battlements and small turrets in each corner.

◆

WOMBOURN
The Canal and Bridge c1965

On the canal near Bratch Locks. The canal is narrow; the maximum dimensions for watercraft are 70ft x 7ft x 3ft draught, with headroom of just 7ft, 6in. It soon found itself at a trading disadvantage. It needed seventy pairs of narrow boats to work the trips carrying coal to Stourport power station.

WOMBOURN, BRATCH LOCKS c1965 W323009

WOMBOURN, THE CANAL AND BRIDGE c1965 W323004

WOMBOURN, HIGH STREET C1965 W323018
Two of the village's attractions are the parish church, which is the only one in the country dedicated to St Benedict Biscop, and the cricket ground, which is one of the few walled-in grounds to survive.

GREAT HAYWOOD, THE TRENT AND MERSEY CANAL C1955 G303011
Great Haywood lies at the junction of the Trent & Mersey with the Staffs & Worcestershire canals. Nearby is Ingestre Hall, the seat of the Earls of Shrewsbury, which was destroyed by fire in 1882 and later rebuilt.

GREAT HAYWOOD, ESSEX BRIDGE c1955 G303019
Essex Bridge was built by the Earls of Essex of Chartley to provide access for hunting parties to Cannock Chase. The original bridge consisted of 42 arches and stretched some way back from the river in order to clear wet ground.

LITTLE HAYWOOD, HIGH STREET c1955 L312002
Along with Great Haywood, this village was where the inhabitants of Shugborough were relocated, as their own village was gradually absorbed into the parkland surrounding Shugborough Hall.

Index

Frith Book Co Titles

www.francisfrith.co.uk

The Frith Book Company publishes over 100 new titles each year. A selection of those currently available are listed below. For latest catalogue please contact Frith Book Co.

Town Books 96 pages, approx 100 photos. County and Themed Books 128 pages, approx 150 photos (unless specified). All titles hardback laminated case and jacket except those indicated pb (paperback)

Title	ISBN	Price	Title	ISBN	Price
Amersham, Chesham & Rickmansworth (pb)			Derby (pb)	1-85937-367-4	£9.99
	1-85937-340-2	£9.99	Derbyshire (pb)	1-85937-196-5	£9.99
Ancient Monuments & Stone Circles	1-85937-143-4	£17.99	Devon (pb)	1-85937-297-x	£9.99
Aylesbury (pb)	1-85937-227-9	£9.99	Dorset (pb)	1-85937-269-4	£9.99
Bakewell	1-85937-113-2	£12.99	Dorset Churches	1-85937-172-8	£17.99
Barnstaple (pb)	1-85937-300-3	£9.99	Dorset Coast (pb)	1-85937-299-6	£9.99
Bath (pb)	1-85937419-0	£9.99	Dorset Living Memories	1-85937-210-4	£14.99
Bedford (pb)	1-85937-205-8	£9.99	Down the Severn	1-85937-118-3	£14.99
Berkshire (pb)	1-85937-191-4	£9.99	Down the Thames (pb)	1-85937-278-3	£9.99
Berkshire Churches	1-85937-170-1	£17.99	Down the Trent	1-85937-311-9	£14.99
Blackpool (pb)	1-85937-382-8	£9.99	Dublin (pb)	1-85937-231-7	£9.99
Bognor Regis (pb)	1-85937-431-x	£9.99	East Anglia (pb)	1-85937-265-1	£9.99
Bournemouth	1-85937-067-5	£12.99	East London	1-85937-080-2	£14.99
Bradford (pb)	1-85937-204-x	£9.99	East Sussex	1-85937-130-2	£14.99
Brighton & Hove(pb)	1-85937-192-2	£8.99	Eastbourne	1-85937-061-6	£12.99
Bristol (pb)	1-85937-264-3	£9.99	Edinburgh (pb)	1-85937-193-0	£8.99
British Life A Century Ago (pb)	1-85937-213-9	£9.99	England in the 1880s	1-85937-331-3	£17.99
Buckinghamshire (pb)	1-85937-200-7	£9.99	English Castles (pb)	1-85937-434-4	£9.99
Camberley (pb)	1-85937-222-8	£9.99	English Country Houses	1-85937-161-2	£17.99
Cambridge (pb)	1-85937-422-0	£9.99	Essex (pb)	1-85937-270-8	£9.99
Cambridgeshire (pb)	1-85937-420-4	£9.99	Exeter	1-85937-126-4	£12.99
Canals & Waterways (pb)	1-85937-291-0	£9.99	Exmoor	1-85937-132-9	£14.99
Canterbury Cathedral (pb)	1-85937-179-5	£9.99	Falmouth	1-85937-066-7	£12.99
Cardiff (pb)	1-85937-093-4	£9.99	Folkestone (pb)	1-85937-124-8	£9.99
Carmarthenshire	1-85937-216-3	£14.99	Glasgow (pb)	1-85937-190-6	£9.99
Chelmsford (pb)	1-85937-310-0	£9.99	Gloucestershire	1-85937-102-7	£14.99
Cheltenham (pb)	1-85937-095-0	£9.99	Great Yarmouth (pb)	1-85937-426-3	£9.99
Cheshire (pb)	1-85937-271-6	£9.99	Greater Manchester (pb)	1-85937-266-x	£9.99
Chester	1-85937-090-x	£12.99	Guildford (pb)	1-85937-410-7	£9.99
Chesterfield	1-85937-378-x	£9.99	Hampshire (pb)	1-85937-279-1	£9.99
Chichester (pb)	1-85937-228-7	£9.99	Hampshire Churches (pb)	1-85937-207-4	£9.99
Colchester (pb)	1-85937-188-4	£8.99	Harrogate	1-85937-423-9	£9.99
Cornish Coast	1-85937-163-9	£14.99	Hastings & Bexhill (pb)	1-85937-131-0	£9.99
Cornwall (pb)	1-85937-229-5	£9.99	Heart of Lancashire (pb)	1-85937-197-3	£9.99
Cornwall Living Memories	1-85937-248-1	£14.99	Helston (pb)	1-85937-214-7	£9.99
Cotswolds (pb)	1-85937-230-9	£9.99	Hereford (pb)	1-85937-175-2	£9.99
Cotswolds Living Memories	1-85937-255-4	£14.99	Herefordshire	1-85937-174-4	£14.99
County Durham	1-85937-123-x	£14.99	Hertfordshire (pb)	1-85937-247-3	£9.99
Croydon Living Memories	1-85937-162-0	£9.99	Horsham (pb)	1-85937-432-8	£9.99
Cumbria	1-85937-101-9	£14.99	Humberside	1-85937-215-5	£14.99
Dartmoor	1-85937-145-0	£14.99	Hythe, Romney Marsh & Ashford	1-85937-256-2	£9.99

Available from your local bookshop or from the publisher

Frith Book Co Titles (continued)

Ipswich (pb)	1-85937-424-7	£9.99	St Ives (pb)	1-85937415-8	£9.99
Ireland (pb)	1-85937-181-7	£9.99	Scotland (pb)	1-85937-182-5	£9.99
Isle of Man (pb)	1-85937-268-6	£9.99	Scottish Castles (pb)	1-85937-323-2	£9.99
Isles of Scilly	1-85937-136-1	£14.99	Sevenoaks & Tunbridge	1-85937-057-8	£12.99
Isle of Wight (pb)	1-85937-429-8	£9.99	Sheffield, South Yorks (pb)	1-85937-267-8	£9.99
Isle of Wight Living Memories	1-85937-304-6	£14.99	Shrewsbury (pb)	1-85937-325-9	£9.99
Kent (pb)	1-85937-189-2	£9.99	Shropshire (pb)	1-85937-326-7	£9.99
Kent Living Memories	1-85937-125-6	£14.99	Somerset	1-85937-153-1	£14.99
Lake District (pb)	1-85937-275-9	£9.99	South Devon Coast	1-85937-107-8	£14.99
Lancaster, Morecambe & Heysham (pb)	1-85937-233-3	£9.99	South Devon Living Memories	1-85937-168-x	£14.99
Leeds (pb)	1-85937-202-3	£9.99	South Hams	1-85937-220-1	£14.99
Leicester	1-85937-073-x	£12.99	Southampton (pb)	1-85937-427-1	£9.99
Leicestershire (pb)	1-85937-185-x	£9.99	Southport (pb)	1-85937-425-5	£9.99
Lincolnshire (pb)	1-85937-433-6	£9.99	Staffordshire	1-85937-047-0	£12.99
Liverpool & Merseyside (pb)	1-85937-234-1	£9.99	Stratford upon Avon	1-85937-098-5	£12.99
London (pb)	1-85937-183-3	£9.99	Suffolk (pb)	1-85937-221-x	£9.99
Ludlow (pb)	1-85937-176-0	£9.99	Suffolk Coast	1-85937-259-7	£14.99
Luton (pb)	1-85937-235-x	£9.99	Surrey (pb)	1-85937-240-6	£9.99
Maidstone	1-85937-056-x	£14.99	Sussex (pb)	1-85937-184-1	£9.99
Manchester (pb)	1-85937-198-1	£9.99	Swansea (pb)	1-85937-167-1	£9.99
Middlesex	1-85937-158-2	£14.99	Tees Valley & Cleveland	1-85937-211-2	£14.99
New Forest	1-85937-128-0	£14.99	Thanet (pb)	1-85937-116-7	£9.99
Newark (pb)	1-85937-366-6	£9.99	Tiverton (pb)	1-85937-178-7	£9.99
Newport, Wales (pb)	1-85937-258-9	£9.99	Torbay	1-85937-063-2	£12.99
Newquay (pb)	1-85937-421-2	£9.99	Truro	1-85937-147-7	£12.99
Norfolk (pb)	1-85937-195-7	£9.99	Victorian and Edwardian Cornwall	1-85937-252-x	£14.99
Norfolk Living Memories	1-85937-217-1	£14.99	Victorian & Edwardian Devon	1-85937-253-8	£14.99
Northamptonshire	1-85937-150-7	£14.99	Victorian & Edwardian Kent	1-85937-149-3	£14.99
Northumberland Tyne & Wear (pb)	1-85937-281-3	£9.99	Vic & Ed Maritime Album	1-85937-144-2	£17.99
North Devon Coast	1-85937-146-9	£14.99	Victorian and Edwardian Sussex	1-85937-157-4	£14.99
North Devon Living Memories	1-85937-261-9	£14.99	Victorian & Edwardian Yorkshire	1-85937-154-x	£14.99
North London	1-85937-206-6	£14.99	Victorian Seaside	1-85937-159-0	£17.99
North Wales (pb)	1-85937-298-8	£9.99	Villages of Devon (pb)	1-85937-293-7	£9.99
North Yorkshire (pb)	1-85937-236-8	£9.99	Villages of Kent (pb)	1-85937-294-5	£9.99
Norwich (pb)	1-85937-194-9	£8.99	Villages of Sussex (pb)	1-85937-295-3	£9.99
Nottingham (pb)	1-85937-324-0	£9.99	Warwickshire (pb)	1-85937-203-1	£9.99
Nottinghamshire (pb)	1-85937-187-6	£9.99	Welsh Castles (pb)	1-85937-322-4	£9.99
Oxford (pb)	1-85937-411-5	£9.99	West Midlands (pb)	1-85937-289-9	£9.99
Oxfordshire (pb)	1-85937-430-1	£9.99	West Sussex	1-85937-148-5	£14.99
Peak District (pb)	1-85937-280-5	£9.99	West Yorkshire (pb)	1-85937-201-5	£9.99
Penzance	1-85937-069-1	£12.99	Weymouth (pb)	1-85937-209-0	£9.99
Peterborough (pb)	1-85937-219-8	£9.99	Wiltshire (pb)	1-85937-277-5	£9.99
Piers	1-85937-237-6	£17.99	Wiltshire Churches (pb)	1-85937-171-x	£9.99
Plymouth	1-85937-119-1	£12.99	Wiltshire Living Memories	1-85937-245-7	£14.99
Poole & Sandbanks (pb)	1-85937-251-1	£9.99	Winchester (pb)	1-85937-428-x	£9.99
Preston (pb)	1-85937-212-0	£9.99	Windmills & Watermills	1-85937-242-2	£17.99
Reading (pb)	1-85937-238-4	£9.99	Worcester (pb)	1-85937-165-5	£9.99
Romford (pb)	1-85937-319-4	£9.99	Worcestershire	1-85937-152-3	£14.99
Salisbury (pb)	1-85937-239-2	£9.99	York (pb)	1-85937-199-x	£9.99
Scarborough (pb)	1-85937-379-8	£9.99	Yorkshire (pb)	1-85937-186-8	£9.99
St Albans (pb)	1-85937-341-0	£9.99	Yorkshire Living Memories	1-85937-166-3	£14.99

See Frith books on the internet www.francisfrith.co.uk

FRITH PRODUCTS & SERVICES

Francis Frith would doubtless be pleased to know that the pioneering publishing venture he started in 1860 still continues today. A hundred and forty years later, The Francis Frith Collection continues in the same innovative tradition and is now one of the foremost publishers of vintage photographs in the world. Some of the current activities include:

Interior Decoration

Today Frith's photographs can be seen framed and as giant wall murals in thousands of pubs, restaurants, hotels, banks, retail stores and other public buildings throughout the country. In every case they enhance the unique local atmosphere of the places they depict and provide reminders of gentler days in an increasingly busy and frenetic world.

Product Promotions

Frith products are used by many major companies to promote the sales of their own products or to reinforce their own history and heritage. Frith promotions have been used by Hovis bread, Courage beers, Scots Porage Oats, Colman's mustard, Cadbury's foods, Mellow Birds coffee, Dunhill pipe tobacco, Guinness, and Bulmer's Cider.

Genealogy and Family History

As the interest in family history and roots grows world-wide, more and more people are turning to Frith's photographs of Great Britain for images of the towns, villages and streets where their ancestors lived; and, of course, photographs of the churches and chapels where their ancestors were christened, married and buried are an essential part of every genealogy tree and family album.

Frith Products

All Frith photographs are available Framed or just as Mounted Prints and Posters (size 23 x 16 inches). These may be ordered from the address below. From time to time other products - Address Books, Calendars, Table Mats, etc - are available.

The Internet

Already twenty thousand Frith photographs can be viewed and purchased on the internet through the Frith websites and a myriad of partner sites.

For more detailed information on Frith companies and products, look at these sites:

www.francisfrith.co.uk
www.francisfrith.com
(for North American visitors)

See the complete list of Frith Books at:

www.francisfrith.co.uk

This web site is regularly updated with the latest list of publications from the Frith Book Company. If you wish to buy books relating to another part of the country that your local bookshop does not stock, you may purchase on-line.

For further information, trade, or author enquiries please contact us at the address below:
The Francis Frith Collection, Frith's Barn, Teffont, Salisbury, Wiltshire, England SP3 5QP.
Tel: +44 (0)1722 716 376 Fax: +44 (0)1722 716 881 Email: sales@francisfrith.co.uk

See Frith books on the internet www.francisfrith.co.uk